Fruitfulness

Dag Heward-Mills

Parchment House

FRUITFULNESS

Copyright © 2022 Dag Heward-Mills

Published by Parchment House 2022
1st Printing 2022

Find out more about Dag Heward-Mills
Healing Jesus Campaign
Write to: evangelist@daghewardmills.org
Website: www.daghewardmills.org
Facebook: Dag Heward-Mills
Twitter: @EvangelistDag

ISBN: 978-1-64330-520-2

Contents

1. God's Purpose for Your Life is Fruitfulness 1

2. You Are Recognized by Fruits 7

3. When God Expects the Fruit 10

4. "I Come Seeking Fruit" 14

5. Jesus' Laws of Fruitfulness 22

6. Cursed for Being Fruitless 30

7. Bearing Tares 33

8. Supernatural Laws of Fruitfulness 36

9. The Rules of Peace and Fruitfulness 44

10. The Holy Spirit Makes You A Fruitful Field 48

11. Enemies of Fruitfulness 53

12. Sacrifice: The Key to Fruitfulness 57

13. Don't Waste Your Goods! 59

CHAPTER 1

God's Purpose for Your Life is Fruitfulness

Ye have not chosen me, but I have chosen you, and ordained you, THAT YE SHOULD GO AND BRING FORTH FRUIT, and that your fruit should remain: that whatsoever ye shall ask of the Father in my name, he may give it you.

John 15:16

God's eternal purpose for you is that you should be fruitful. To be fruitful is God's purpose for you. God sees you as a tree that must bear fruit. To be fruitful means to be full of fruits and products worthy of all the investments that have been made in you.

To be fruitful means to be abundant, abounding, blooming and blossoming.

To be fruitful means to flourish, to become plenteous and to proliferate. To be fruitful means to produce a lot and to breed. God wants you to produce a lot and God wants you to bear fruits.

If you study the lives of the different people whom God called and appointed, you will notice that He called and appointed them to fruitfulness. Jesus told His disciples the reason why He had chosen and ordained them. He had chosen and ordained them to go and bring forth fruit, nothing else. You are a tree that God has planted and He is expecting fruit from you.

God is looking for something from you. It is important that you live your life fulfilling His will and not yours. Every single one of the patriarchs was called to be fruitful. The purpose of the call of God is always *fruitfulness*.

Adam was called to be fruitful! God blessed him so that he would be fruitful. God's purpose was to fill the earth with human beings. Even up till now, vast sections of the planet have no human life. God had a plan to cover the earth with human beings.

Abraham was called to be exceedingly fruitful! God wanted a special group of people that He called His own. He wanted an obedient person to bring forth a large group of obedient children.

Isaac was also called to fruitfulness! Indeed, he carried on in the same line as his father, Abraham. The blessing of fruitfulness was to be passed from Abraham to Isaac.

Jacob was called to be fruitful! Jacob received a blessing from his father. And the blessing was to multiply and to be fruitful. Jacob had many children and began to manifest the fruitfulness that Abraham had been called to.

Rebekah was called to be fruitful! Rebekah was commissioned to become the mother of thousands of millions. This is the purpose of God! Your fruitfulness is what God is looking for.

Israel was called to be fruitful! When the nation of Israel lived in Goshen, they were fruitful, and increased abundantly, and multiplied, and waxed exceeding mighty; and the land was filled with them. Their population swelled and the fruitfulness of Israel was manifested.

Ishmael was called to be fruitful! Even Ishmael, who was Isaac's brother, was blessed to become twelve princes.

Joseph was blessed to be fruitful! Joseph's blessing was to be a fruitful bough. His children, Manasseh and Ephraim received a blessing and commission to become fruitful.

Christians are called to be fruitful! The plan of God is that believers would follow in this spirit of fruitfulness. We are to walk worthy of God's calling by being fruitful. It is time to walk in the fruitfulness, the productivity, the abundance, the soul winning, the church planting, the blossoming, the breeding and the multiplying grace that is upon every believer.

The Vision for Fruitfulness in Scripture

1. God's purpose for Adam was fruitfulness.

So God created man in his own image, in the image of God created he him; male and female created he them.
AND GOD BLESSED THEM, AND GOD SAID UNTO THEM, BE FRUITFUL, and multiply, and replenish the earth, and subdue it: and have dominion over the fish of

the sea, and over the fowl of the air, and over every living thing that moveth upon the earth.

Genesis 1:27-28

2. God's purpose for Abraham was fruitfulness.

As for me, behold, my covenant is with thee, and thou shalt be a father of many nations. Neither shall thy name any more be called Abram, but thy name shall be Abraham; for a father of many nations have I made thee. And I WILL MAKE THEE EXCEEDING FRUITFUL, and I will make nations of thee, and kings shall come out of thee.

Genesis 17:4-6

3. God's purpose for Isaac was fruitfulness.

And there was a famine in the land, beside the first famine that was in the days of Abraham. And Isaac went unto Abimelech king of the Philistines unto Gerar.

And the Lord appeared unto him, and said, Go not down into Egypt; dwell in the land which I shall tell thee of: Sojourn in this land, and I will be with thee, and will bless thee; for unto thee, and unto thy seed, I will give all these countries, and I will perform the oath which I sware unto Abraham thy father; AND I WILL MAKE THY SEED TO MULTIPLY AS THE STARS OF HEAVEN, and will give unto thy seed all these countries; and in thy seed shall all the nations of the earth be blessed;

Genesis 26:1-4

4. God's purpose for Jacob was fruitfulness.

And Isaac called Jacob, and blessed him, and charged him, and said unto him, Thou shalt not take a wife of the daughters of Canaan. Arise, go to Padanaram, to the house of Bethuel thy mother's father; and take thee a wife from thence of the daughters of Laban thy mother's brother. AND GOD ALMIGHTY BLESS THEE, AND MAKE THEE FRUITFUL, AND MULTIPLY THEE, THAT

THOU MAYEST BE A MULTITUDE OF PEOPLE; and give thee the blessing of Abraham, to thee, and to thy seed with thee; that thou mayest inherit the land wherein thou art a stranger, which God gave unto Abraham.

Genesis 28:1-4

5. God's purpose for Joseph was fruitfulness.

JOSEPH IS A FRUITFUL BOUGH, even a fruitful bough by a well; whose branches run over the wall: the archers have sorely grieved him, and shot at him, and hated him: But his bow abode in strength, and the arms of his hands were made strong by the hands of the mighty God of Jacob; (from thence is the shepherd, the stone of Israel:) Even by the God of thy father, who shall help thee; and by the Almighty, who shall bless thee with blessings of heaven above, blessings of the deep that lieth under, blessings of the breasts, and of the womb:

The blessings of thy father have prevailed above the blessings of my progenitors unto the utmost bound of the everlasting hills: they shall be on the head of Joseph, and on the crown of the head of him that was separate from his brethren.

Genesis 49:22-26

6. God's purpose for Manasseh and Ephraim was fruitfulness.

AND JOSEPH TOOK THEM BOTH, EPHRAIM IN HIS RIGHT HAND TOWARD ISRAEL'S LEFT HAND, AND MANASSEH IN HIS LEFT HAND TOWARD ISRAEL'S RIGHT HAND, and brought them near unto him. And Israel stretched out his right hand, and laid it upon Ephraim's head, who was the younger, and his left hand upon Manasseh's head, guiding his hands wittingly; for Manasseh was the firstborn.

And he blessed Joseph, and said, God, before whom my fathers Abraham and Isaac did walk, the God which fed me all my life long unto this day, The Angel which redeemed me from all evil, bless the lads; and let my name be named on them, and the name of my fathers Abraham and Isaac; AND LET THEM GROW INTO A MULTITUDE IN THE MIDST OF THE EARTH.

Genesis 48:13-16

7. God's purpose for Rebekah was fruitfulness.

And they blessed Rebekah, and said unto her, THOU ART OUR SISTER, BE THOU THE MOTHER OF THOUSANDS OF MILLIONS, and let thy seed possess the gate of those which hate them.

Genesis 24:60

8. God's purpose for Ishmael was fruitfulness.

And as for Ishmael, I have heard thee: Behold, I have blessed him, and will make him fruitful, and WILL MULTIPLY HIM EXCEEDINGLY; TWELVE PRINCES SHALL HE BEGET, and I will make him a great nation.

Genesis 17:20

9. God's purpose for Israel was fruitfulness.

And Joseph died, and all his brethren, and all that generation. AND THE CHILDREN OF ISRAEL WERE FRUITFUL, AND INCREASED ABUNDANTLY, AND MULTIPLIED, AND WAXED EXCEEDING MIGHTY; AND THE LAND WAS FILLED WITH THEM.

Exodus 1:6-7

10. God's purpose for the believer is fruitfulness.

That ye might walk worthy of the Lord unto all pleasing, BEING FRUITFUL in every good work, and increasing in the knowledge of God;

Colossians 1:10

CHAPTER 2

You Are Recognized by Fruits

For a good tree bringeth not forth corrupt fruit; neither doth a corrupt tree bring forth good fruit. FOR EVERY TREE IS KNOWN BY HIS OWN FRUIT. For of thorns men do not gather figs, nor of a bramble bush gather they grapes.

Luke 6:43-44

YE SHALL KNOW THEM BY THEIR FRUITS. Do men gather grapes of thorns, or figs of thistles? Even so every good tree bringeth forth good fruit; but a corrupt tree bringeth forth evil fruit. A good tree cannot bring forth evil fruit, neither can a corrupt tree bring forth good fruit. Every tree that bringeth not forth good fruit is hewn down, and cast into the fire. Wherefore by their fruits ye shall know them.

Matthew 7:16-20

1. You are identified by your fruits.

Once you see the mangoes on a tree, you know that it is a mango tree. Your fruits tell us what kind of tree you are. A good tree brings forth good fruits and a bad tree brings forth bad fruits.

A good person brings forth good things. I know who Adolf Hitler is when I see that he caused the deaths of fifty million people through the wars that he started. I know what kind of person you are when I see the happy husband or wife that you have. I know the kind of person you are when I see your happy employees.

Your disgruntled, critical, murmuring staff members reveal a lot about you. We know that you are a good tree because of your good fruits. Your fruits give you away. Your fruits reveal a lot about you. Without even talking to you, we know a whole lot about you because of your fruits.

2. You are evaluated by your fruits.

People are best assessed by the fruits that they bear. Your life is known and understood by the fruits that you bear. It is impossible to bear certain fruits if you are not part of that tree. It is impossible for an orange tree to bear apples. No matter the speeches, the explanations you make, your fruits reveal who you really are. African leaders have all sorts of speeches and arguments to make about the state of the countries they lead. But the fruits of their leadership reveal who they really are. The poor and backward state of affairs in most African nations are the fruits of deficient leadership. The fruits tell us all we need to know. The fruits tell us that incapable men are at the helm of affairs in many nations.

Your fruits reveal who you really are. I know who you are when I see the souls that you have won to the Lord.

From the attendance of your church, I know who you are.

From the income of your church, I know who you are.

From the crusades that you have, I know who you are.

From the books that you write, I know who you are.

The church that you pastor tells us all we need to know.

3. You are a mystery without fruits.

When a tree has no fruits, it is difficult to tell what kind of tree it is. When a tree has no fruits, it is difficult to tell what you are dealing with. Is it a mango tree? Is it an olive tree? Is it an orange tree? The mystery around you multiplies when there is no fruit from your life. When a tree has no fruit, it must be thrown into the fire. Watch out for people who do not bear fruits. You must get them out of your life. They are mysterious and dangerous.

You will be thrown into the fire if you do not produce what God is expecting. You can avoid the fire by bearing fruits unto the Lord. What are the fruits that God wants from you? God wants souls! God wants churches! God wants good works that He has ordained. God deals with us on the basis of our fruits.

Life and death depend on the fruits that you have. Once the tree does not produce good fruits, it will be cut down and thrown into the fire. Expect the fire if you do not bear fruits!

CHAPTER 3

When God Expects the Fruit

He spake also this parable; A certain man had a fig tree planted in his vineyard; and he came and sought fruit thereon, and found none. Then said he unto the dresser of his vineyard, Behold, these three years I come seeking fruit on this fig tree, and find none: cut it down; why cumbereth it the ground? And he answering said unto him, Lord, let it alone THIS YEAR also, till I shall dig about it, and dung it: And if it bear fruit, well: and if not, then after that thou shalt cut it down.

Luke 13:6-9

There is a time when you are expected to bring forth fruits. We cannot wait endlessly for you to bear the fruits that God expects. There is a time for fruitfulness. In this chapter, I want you to see that the timing of your fruitfulness is very important.

1. God expects fruits within a year.

He spake also this parable; A certain man had a fig tree planted in his vineyard; and he came and sought fruit thereon, and found none. Then said he unto the dresser of his vine-yard, Behold, these three years I come seeking fruit on this fig tree, and find none: cut it down; why cumbereth it the ground? And he answering said unto him, LORD, LET IT ALONE THIS YEAR ALSO, TILL I SHALL DIG ABOUT IT, AND DUNG IT: AND IF IT BEAR FRUIT, WELL: AND IF NOT, THEN AFTER THAT THOU SHALT CUT IT DOWN.

Luke 13:6-9

There are certain things we must see within a year. If we do not see a certain change within a year, then there will be no change in the future. No one can wait endlessly for lunch. There is a time to eat and there is a time for other things. Many restaurants close by 3.00pm for lunch. If you are not there, you lose your chance for lunch. In the same way, God cannot wait endlessly for you to produce fruit for Him to enjoy. Within a year, there must be some fruit! Certain changes must take place within a year. When there is no change in a year's time, it is time to take decisions. Hard decisions must be taken to cut down certain fruitless trees after one year.

2. God expects fruits within three months.

So David brought not the ark home to himself to the city of David, but carried it aside into the house of Obededom the Gittite. AND THE ARK OF GOD REMAINED WITH THE FAMILY OF OBEDEDOM IN HIS HOUSE THREE

MONTHS. AND THE LORD BLESSED THE HOUSE
OF OBEDEDOM, AND ALL THAT HE HAD.

1 Chronicles 13:13-14

There are certain changes we must see within three months.
If we do not see a certain change within three months, then we
know for sure that there will be no change in the future. When
the Ark of the Covenant visited Obededom's house, there was
a drastic change within three months. Within three months
everybody knew that something unusual was happening. There
are certain fruits that must be borne within three months. In
most relationships, if there is no change in three months there
is not likely to be any change ever. After a counselling session,
you expect changes to take place. We cannot wait endlessly for
a change that never comes. You may safely conclude that there
will never be a change if certain changes do not take place within
three months.

3. God expects fruits within five years.

And when ye shall come into the land, and shall have
planted all manner of trees for food, then ye shall count
the fruit thereof as uncircumcised: three years shall it be
as uncircum-cised unto you: it shall not be eaten of. But in
the fourth year all the fruit thereof shall be holy to praise
the Lord withal. And IN THE FIFTH YEAR SHALL YE
EAT OF THE FRUIT THEREOF, that it may yield unto
you the increase thereof: I am the Lord your God.

Leviticus 19:23-25

There are some fruits that are borne only after five years.
Just like Chinese bamboo, many churches develop properly only
after five years of being planted in the ground. After planting the
Chinese bamboo in the ground, you need to water and fertilize
it for five years. All through the five years, you will see nothing
at all for all your labour. The bamboo shoot does not even come
out of the ground within the first five years. However, in the fifth
year the Chinese bamboo will break through the ground, and in

six weeks it will grow to over ninety feet tall. Indeed, without faith you will stop watering the Chinese bamboo. If at any time you stop watering the bamboo during the five years, it will die in the ground and you will have no fruit. The Chinese bamboo is a revelation of fruit you can bear only after five years.

There are fruits you can expect to see only after five years. There will be little to see after one year, two years or even three years.

Indeed, a certain kind of church growth is only seen after five years. You will see certain fruits only after five years of ministry. Many pastors develop in their ministries only after five years of real ministry. Perhaps, there is a major leap forward in your ministry every five years.

CHAPTER 4

"I Come Seeking Fruit"

He spake also this parable; A certain man had a fig tree planted in his vineyard; and he came and sought fruit thereon, and found none.

Then said he unto the dresser of his vineyard, BEHOLD, THESE THREE YEARS I COME SEEKING FRUIT on this fig tree, and find none: cut it down; why cumbereth it the ground?

And he answering said unto him, Lord, let it alone this year also, till I shall dig about it, and dung it: And if it bear fruit, well: and if not, then after that thou shalt cut it down.

Luke 13:6-9

G od is coming your way looking for fruits! God is expecting to find fruits when He comes. Do not let Him be disappointed. When someone has invested in you, he expects to reap the fruits of his investment.

All through the Bible, you see examples of God coming in search of fruit from you. You also see examples of human beings who were expecting fruit and did not receive them.

People's reaction to those who do not bear fruit is often unpleasant. The reaction to those who yield up negativity instead of yielding good fruit is even more negative. The statement "I come seeking fruit" came from Jesus. Let us pay proper respect to His words, "I come seeking fruit."

Jesus is coming seeking fruit from you and me. I want you to notice the negative reactions to those who do not have fruit.

1. I COME SEEKING FRUIT FROM THE EARTH

There is a curse for the earth that does not bring forth fruits when expected. After someone has sowed into your life and invested great things, he expects to receive some good fruit. Do not yield up negativity and evil things in response to all the good that has been done for you. Do not speak against the one who has loved you. Do not speak negatively behind someone's back in exchange for his love. Jesus said, "He who speaks against the Holy Spirit will never be for-given" (Mark 3:29). Speaking negatively is an evil fruit that you can bear. Do not allow yourself to fall into the curse of speaking negatively about someone who has cared for you and loved you. Speaking against your father behind his back is a negative seed that has a strong response in the spirit.

> For the earth which drinketh in the rain that cometh oft upon it, and bringeth forth herbs meet for them by whom it is dressed, receiveth blessing from God: But that which beareth thorns and briers is rejected, and is nigh unto cursing; whose end is to be burned. But, beloved, we are

persuaded better things of you, and things that accompany salvation, though we thus speak

Hebrews 6:7-9

2. I COME SEEKING FRUIT FROM MEN WE FOUGHT FOR

Gideon fought for the men of Shechem. How did they repay him? How did they reward Gideon for his great effort? Gideon risked his life several times for these people. They repaid him by killing seventy of his children. There are many curses that will always be fulfilled because you cannot break the laws of God and expect to get away scot-free.

Gideon reaped the fruit of mass murder and the massacre of his family.

The curse of Jotham, the youngest son of Jerubbaal (Gideon), on the men of Shechem came to pass because they repaid good with evil. The men of Shechem bore evil fruits.

Jotham delivered a curse to the tree that bore evil fruits, "My father fought for you, and adventured his life far, and delivered you out of the hand of Midian: And ye are risen up against my father's house this day, and have slain his sons, threescore and ten persons, upon one stone." They repaid the goodness of Gideon by killing seventy of his children. This was not the fruit Gideon was expecting after all he had done for the people of Israel.

And the bramble said unto the trees, If in truth ye anoint me king over you, then come and put your trust in my shadow: and if not, let fire come out of the bramble, and devour the cedars of Lebanon. Now therefore, if ye have done truly and sincerely, in that ye have made Abimelech king, and if ye have dealt well with Jerubbaal and his house, and have done unto him according to the deserving of his hands; (For my father fought for you, and adventured his life far, and delivered you out of the hand of Midian: And ye are risen up against my father's house this day, and have slain his sons, threescore and ten persons, upon one stone, and have made Abimelech, the son of his maidservant, king over the men of Shechem, because he is your brother;) If ye then have dealt truly and sincerely with Jerubbaal and with his house this day, then rejoice ye in Abimelech, and let him also rejoice in you: But if not, let fire come out from Abimelech, and devour the men of Shechem, and the house of Millo; and let fire come out from the men of Shechem, and from the house of Millo, and devour Abimelech. And Jotham ran away, and fled, and went to Beer, and dwelt there, for fear of Abimelech his brother.

Judges 9:15-21

3. I COME SEEKING FRUIT FROM PROSPEROUS MEN

David came seeking fruit from Nabal. He had looked after Nabal's flocks and provided security throughout the year. All he wanted was a few lambs that he could roast with his men. Nabal denied him this little privilege and insulted him.

David's reaction to this evil fruit was instant. He gathered his men with the intention of slaughtering Nabal and his household.

And Samuel died; and all the Israelites were gathered together, and lamented him, and buried him in his house at Ramah. And David arose, and went down to the wilderness of Paran. And there was a man in Maon, whose possessions were in Carmel; and the man was very great, and he had three thousand sheep, and a thousand goats: and he was shearing his sheep in Carmel. Now the name of the man was Nabal; and the name of his wife Abigail: and she was a woman of good understanding, and of a beautiful countenance: but the man was churlish and evil in his doings; and he was of the house of Caleb.

And David heard in the wilderness that Nabal did shear his sheep. And David sent out ten young men, and David said unto the young men, Get you up to Carmel, and go to Nabal, and greet him in my name: And thus shall ye say to him that liveth in prosperity, Peace be both to thee, and peace be to thine house, and peace be unto all that thou hast. And now I have heard that thou hast shearers: now thy shepherds which were with us, we hurt them not, neither was there ought missing unto them, all the while they were in Carmel. Ask thy young men, and they will shew thee.

Wherefore let the young men find favour in thine eyes: for we come in a good day: give, I pray thee, whatsoever cometh to thine hand unto thy servants, and to thy son David. And when David's young men came, they spake to Nabal according to all those words in the name of David, and ceased.

1 Samuel 25:1-9

God often comes to us seeking fruit in the time of prosperity. He has protected us, helped us and delivered us from many evils that we do not know about. There are times He expects us to say "Thank you" with a big offering and a big gift. If He gets insults instead of thanksgiving, what do you think His reaction will be?

Jesus said, He that speaks against the Holy Spirit would never be forgiven (Mark 3:28-29). This scripture means that speaking against someone can be a sin. Do not speak against people who have loved you and cared for you. You will be committing a sin.

4. I COME SEEKING FRUIT FROM MY SON

Isaac was seeking fruit from his son. Isaac was not expecting deception and wickedness from his son, Jacob. He was expecting honesty, goodness and love in exchange for the love that he had shown to his son. All Isaac wanted from his son was some savoury meat. He had looked after his son for many years. He had educated his son and protected him. On that fateful day, Isaac sought some good fruit from his son. When he ate the savoury meat, he released an even greater blessing on his son.

Jacob was afraid to deceive his father because he knew it would bring a curse. Jacob knew that bearing evil fruits would ignite a curse. Deceiving someone who has been good to you brings a curse. A tree is expected to bring forth good fruits and not evil fruits. Jacob's mother diverted this curse to herself. She said, "Let the curse of deceiving your father come upon me." Indeed, we never heard of her again after this statement.

> And it came to pass, that when Isaac was old, and his eyes were dim, so that he could not see, he called Esau his eldest son, and said unto him, My son: and he said unto him, Behold, here am I. And he said, Behold now, I am old, I know not the day of my death: Now therefore take, I pray thee, thy weapons, thy quiver and thy bow, and go out to the field, and take me some venison; And make me savoury meat, such as I love, and bring it to me, that I may eat; that my soul may bless thee before I die. And Rebekah heard when Isaac spake to Esau his son. And Esau went to the field to hunt for venison, and to bring it.
>
> And Rebekah spake unto Jacob her son, saying, Behold, I heard thy father speak unto Esau thy brother, saying, Bring me venison, and make me savoury meat, that I may eat, and bless thee before the Lord before my death. Now therefore, my son, obey my voice according to that which I command thee. Go now to the flock, and fetch me from thence two good kids of the goats; and I will make them savoury meat for thy father, such as he loveth: And thou shalt bring it to thy father, that he may eat, and that he may bless thee before his death. And Jacob said to Rebekah his mother, Behold, Esau my brother is a hairy man, and I am a smooth man: My father peradventure will feel me, and I shall seem to him as a deceiver; and I shall bring a curse upon me, and not a blessing. And his mother said unto him, upon me be thy curse, my son: only obey my voice, and go fetch me them.

Genesis 27:1-13

5. I COME SEEKING FRUIT FROM MEN I HAVE CREATED

God was expecting fruit from His creation. Cain and Abel were the prosperous children of Adam and Eve. Abel brought

God a good fruit of a lamb. Cain gathered some vegetables together and presented them to the Lord.

God was expecting something with life and not some dried leaves. God was expecting something substantial from His creation. Yet, only one Abel felt it was necessary to bring a good fruit to the Lord. This was the beginning of all curses on the earth. Cain opened the door for curses to come into this world and it all happened because he would not give the fruit expected of him.

> And Adam knew Eve his wife; and she conceived, and bare Cain, and said, I have gotten a man from the Lord. And she again bare his brother Abel. And Abel was a keeper of sheep, but Cain was a tiller of the ground. And in process of time it came to pass, that Cain brought of the fruit of the ground an offering unto the Lord. And Abel, he also brought of the firstlings of his flock and of the fat thereof. And the Lord had respect unto Abel and to his offering: But unto Cain and to his offering he had not respect. And Cain was very wroth, and his countenance fell. And the Lord said unto Cain, Why art thou wroth? and why is thy countenance fallen?
>
> Genesis 4:1-6

6. I COME SEEKING FRUIT FROM CHILDREN I HAVE NOURISHED

When children are brought up, good fruit is expected from them. Every parent is expecting a good return for his hard investment. When a child grows up and brings forth rebellion, it can only lead to a curse. Every child must yield good fruit towards his parents. Do not be a rebel! Do not give your parents disobedience, rebellion and a bad attitude!

> The vision of Isaiah the son of Amoz, which he saw concerning Judah and Jerusalem in the days of Uzziah, Jotham, Ahaz, and Hezekiah, kings of Judah. Hear, O heavens, and give ear, O earth: for the Lord hath spoken, I

HAVE NOURISHED AND BROUGHT UP CHILDREN, AND THEY HAVE REBELLED AGAINST ME. The ox knoweth his owner, and the ass his master's crib: but Israel doth not know, my people doth not consider. Ah sinful nation, a people laden with iniquity, a seed of evildoers, children that are corrupters: they have forsaken the Lord, THEY HAVE PROVOKED THE HOLY ONE OF ISRAEL UNTO ANGER, THEY ARE GONE AWAY BACKWARD.

Isaiah 1:1-4

CHAPTER 5

Jesus' Laws of Fruitfulness

I am the true vine, and my Father is the husbandman. Every branch in me that beareth not fruit he taketh away: and every branch that beareth fruit, he purgeth it, that it may bring forth more fruit. Now ye are clean through the word which I have spoken unto you. Abide in me, and I in you. As the branch cannot bear fruit of itself, except it abide in the vine; no more can ye, except ye abide in me. I am the vine, ye are the branches: He that abideth in me, and I in him, the same bringeth forth much fruit: for without me ye can do nothing. If a man abide not in me, he is cast forth as a branch, and is withered; and men gather them, and cast them into the fire, and they are burned. If ye abide in me, and my words abide in you, ye shall ask what ye will, and it shall be done unto you. Herein is my Father glorified, that ye bear much fruit; so shall ye be my disciples.

John 15:1-8

1. **Jesus' first Law of fruitfulness: Fruitless Christians will be taken away.**

   Every branch in me that beareth not fruit he taketh away...John 15:2

   This law means that you will be removed from the higher realms of ministry when you do not bear fruit.

   This law means that you will be taken away from the front line of ministry when you do not bear the fruits expected.

   This law means that you will be sent back into the secular world when you do not bear the fruits expected.

   This law also means that you will die prematurely if you do not bear the expected fruits. Indeed, the lack of fruit in your life could mean the end of your life.

   This law means that you may die suddenly or you may die slowly because you are not bearing the appropriate fruits.

2. **Jesus' second Law of fruitfulness: Fruitful Christians will be purged to make them bear more fruit.**

   Every branch that beareth fruit, he purgeth it, that it may bring forth more fruit.... John 15:2

   Expect purging because you are bearing some good fruits. Purging is a semi-violent process in which unwanted qualities and conditions are removed.   Purging is often abrupt, and sometimes violent. When you are purged, it means you are forced to expel, eject, clear out, dismiss, discharge, eradicate or exclude something from your life.

   Many events in our lives are actually purging processes. Suffering through crises and troubles has a way of clearing out unwanted attitudes, qualities and conditions from our lives.

A marriage may purge you of unwanted pride.

A job may purge you of your arrogance.

An experience and a relationship may purge you of foolishness.

I cannot tell what the purging experience in your life will be like. But you must expect purging as part of your Christian experience. Every fruit-bearing tree needs to be purged of something.

A bad marriage experience may purge you of childhood delusions so that you can bear much fruit.

Do not ask me what exactly is going to happen to you. I can tell you that as long as you are bearing fruit, expect purging that will make you bear even more fruit.

Some of you need to be purged of your family's influence.

Some of you need to be purged of your country's traits and characteristics. The death of someone in your life may serve as a purge to violently remove a negative influence from your life.

3. **Jesus' third Law of fruitfulness: Cleanness and purity are needed for fruit bearing.**

   Now ye are clean through the word which I have spoken unto you.... John 15:3

   Whilst Jesus was sharing about bearing fruit, He spoke of cleanness, purity and holiness. Without removing thorns, thistles and weeds, plants will never grow and will never bear the fruits they are expected to bear. Without holiness you cannot see God.

   Follow peace with all men, and holiness, without which no man shall see the Lord:

   Hebrews 12:14

As Jesus spoke of bearing fruit, I am sure the disciples were thinking to themselves, "We are not good enough to be used by the Lord for such great works." They were certainly not holy men because they all betrayed Christ. But Jesus reassured them that they were made clean by listening to His words. No one is good enough and no one will ever qualify. *You are clean by believing in the word of God that comes to you.*

We are justified by faith. It is not time to go around establishing your own righteousness. It is time to believe when God calls you. You are made clean by believing in the very call of God on your life.

If God has called you, you are clean by the call and the Word that is spoken to you. If the call of God was based on a person's moral qualities and purity, I assure you, few people would ever qualify. Notice how Peter made it clear that he was not a holy or powerful person.

And when Peter saw it, he answered unto the people, Ye men of Israel, why marvel ye at this? or WHY LOOK YE SO EARNESTLY ON US, AS THOUGH BY OUR OWN POWER OR HOLINESS WE HAD MADE THIS MAN TO WALK?

Acts 3:12

Indeed, if you are looking for intrinsic holiness and righteousness, you would not even be able to read the Bible because most of the people who wrote the Bible had serious moral blemishes.

When Abraham believed in God's call, he was clean by the Word that was spoken to him. Because he believed the Word, it was counted to him as righteousness.

Whenever you look at yourself critically, you will feel like hiding. When Adam looked at himself, he ran to hide between the trees because he realised that he was no longer qualified to be near God.

Our fallen state makes us look at ourselves and despise what we see. That is why most human beings have a low self-esteem.

Believe the word of God that has been spoken to you! You are clean and qualified through the Word that has been spoken to you. Are you called by God? That call in itself cleans you up and qualifies you!

4. **Jesus' fourth Law of fruitfulness: Closeness is needed for fruit bearing.**

   ... As the branch cannot bear fruit of itself, except it abide in the vine; no more can ye, except ye abide in me. I am the vine, ye are the branches... John 15:4-5

   It is a law that closeness is required for fruitfulness. A couple cannot bear fruit until they become very close. A married couple cannot have children until their sexual organs become very close. This law cannot be broken. Spiritually speaking, people cannot bear fruit until they become close to God and close to the people whom they are supposed to be close to.

   Closeness is an important spiritual quality to attain. The closer you are to the fire, the warmer you will feel. Over the years, I have noticed that people who are far from the anointing rarely bear much fruit. There is something called "spiritual distance".

   Jesus said to someone, "You are not far from the Kingdom" (Mark 12:34). Obviously, He was not telling the man that he was twenty kilometres from the kingdom of God. He was telling the man that in the spirit he was not far from the kingdom. If a person can be spiritually near the kingdom then he can also be spiritually far from the kingdom.

   It is important to be spiritually close. The vine is supposed to be in the branches and the branches are supposed to be in the vine for fruit to be borne. The closer you get to God, the closer you are to the anointing, the closer you are to the anointed, the closer you will be to bearing fruit!

How can a man be close to God? Very simple! Draw nigh to God and He will draw nigh to you (James 4:8). When you take time to draw nigh to God, He will draw nigh to you. People who take time to go and wait on the Lord experience the beauty of His presence. A person who has the presence of God with him is usually bearing much fruit. Spend time drawing near to God!

5. **Jesus' fifth Law of fruitfulness: Abiding in Christ is essential for fruitfulness.**

He that abideth in me, and I in him, the same bringeth forth much fruit ... John 15:5

Abiding in Christ means staying in God. So many people are in and out of God. Today, their hearts are committed! Tomorrow they are not so committed! It is important to stay committed. If you have been a Christian for three continuous years, I believe you are abiding in Christ. As you abide in Him and He abides in you, you will bear much fruit.

The longer you stay in God, the more fruitful you become. It is easier to bear fruit after staying in God for some time. If God has called you, stay with your conviction and do not waver. The longer you abide in your convictions, the more fruitful you will be. Experienced long-standing pastors who have been abiding in Christ, are able to generate a larger church much faster than a young inexperienced pastor. This is because they have been abiding in Christ much longer.

6. **Jesus' sixth Law of fruitfulness: Slow deterioration and withering is the sign of those who no longer bear fruit.**

If a man abide not in me, he is cast forth as a branch, and is withered; and men gather them, and cast them into the fire, and they are burned.... John 15:6

Withering is a process where you change gradually. You lose lustre! You lose the freshness! You decay and change and deteriorate! If you look closely at many once-famous ministries, you will notice a slight withering and decaying in many of them.

It takes a trained eye to notice withering when it is happening. Withering is a very important feature to watch out for and to look out for.

Withering is a sign that fruitfulness has ended.

Withering is a sign that the presence is gone.

Withering is also a sign that people are not abiding in God as they used to.

Withering is a sign that the presence of God is no longer there.

The more spiritual you are, the more you will notice withering in pastors and even in ordinary Christians.

7. **Jesus' seventh Law of fruitfulness: Fruit-bearers are guaranteed answers to their prayers.**

If ye abide in me, and my words abide in you, ye shall ask what ye will, and it shall be done unto you.... John 15:7

Whilst Jesus was speaking about bearing fruit, He guaranteed answers to prayers. When you are into fruit-bearing, you can expect guaranteed answers to your prayers. Even we, who are evil, do not respond favourably to our rebellious children. When a child is disobedient, you are less likely to give your good things to that child. Do you think God gives His good things to rebellious children? Certainly not! He gives His good things to those who are obedient and who bear good fruit. Indeed, if you abide in Him you can expect to receive a hundred per cent answers to your prayers!

Fruitful believers are not likely to ask for unnecessary things. If you look at Paul, one of the most fruitful apostles, you will notice how he prayed for the Spirit of revelation and wisdom. He also prayed that the eyes of his understanding would be enlightened (Ephesians 1: 17-18). These are the kinds of prayer topics that fruitful Christians pray. If a fruitful Christian were to ask for a car, I am sure his answer would be forthcoming very quickly. It is time to become a fruit-bearing Christian because the advantages of being fruitful are so great. God will answer your prayers because you are a fruit-bearing Christian. This is the seventh law of fruitfulness.

8. **Jesus' eighth Law of fruitfulness: Fruit-bearing makes God very happy with you.**

   Herein is my Father glorified, that ye bear much fruit; so shall ye be my disciples. John 15:8

   What exactly does it mean to glorify God? To glorify God is to bear much fruit. Many Christians are happy and content to bear little fruit in the ministry. Most Christians just want to be rich. They want to have everything this world offers. The hearts of many Christians are simply not directed towards glorifying God.

   Many people are simply not interested in bearing fruits so that they can glorify God. But when you do glorify God, He will honour you and give you great things.

CHAPTER 6

Cursed for Being Fruitless

And on the morrow, when they were come from Bethany, he was hungry: And seeing a fig tree afar off having leaves, he came, if haply he might find any thing thereon: and when he came to it, he found nothing but leaves; for the time of figs was not yet. And Jesus answered and said unto it, NO MAN EAT FRUIT OF THEE HEREAFTER FOR EVER. And his disciples heard it. ... And in the morning, as they passed by, they saw the fig tree dried up from the roots.

Mark 11:12-14, 20

I have a mango tree in my house that has not borne me any fruit. The truth is that I do not eat mango leaves. I do not enjoy mango leaves! I do not eat mango leaf salad! I do not eat the bark of the mango tree. The only part of the mango tree that I eat is the fruit.

Since I carried the mango tree from Guinea to Ghana, I have watered and protected it in my house but it has not given me even one fruit. My anger may soon be directed at this tree because it is not giving me anything that I like.

What does God want from you? Does Jesus want the Coca Cola in your fridge? Does God want to eat your salad? Does God want the meat in your soup? Does God want your shoes? Does God want your clothes?

Indeed, God does not want any of these things from you. God requires fruit! If God has invested something in your life, He expects to get the fruits of it from you.

Does He want your money? Does He want your time? Does He want souls? Does He want churches?

There is indeed a curse for fruitlessness. When Jesus came to the fig tree and found no fruit on it, He cursed it! When Jesus comes to you expecting fruits, you better have the fruits that He is expecting from you. You may receive a withering curse because you are not bearing fruits worthy of your salvation. Do you want Jesus to speak a word into your life that causes you to wither and vanish out of this world? Then rise up and bear the fruits that correspond to the goodness that God has shown you.

God is expecting something from you! His purpose for saving you is that you bear fruit.

Why did He save you? Why did He choose you? Why did He rescue you from the world? He saved you so that you would save others! He loved you so that you would love others! He cared for you so that you would care for others! You need to bring forth fruits that are worthy of your repentance and your salvation.

31

But when he saw many of the Pharisees and Sadducees come to his baptism, he said unto them, O generation of vipers, who hath warned you to flee from the wrath to come? BRING FORTH THEREFORE FRUITS MEET FOR REPENTANCE: And think not to say within yourselves, we have Abraham to our father: for I say unto you, that God is able of these stones to raise up children unto Abraham. And now also the axe is laid unto the root of the trees: therefore every tree which bringeth not forth good fruit is hewn down, and cast into the fire.

Matthew 3:7-10

There is nothing much that you can do for God. God has loved us! How can we say thanks? How can you say thanks for your salvation? By obeying the words of Jesus and going into the whole world to preach the gospel of Jesus! God is expecting appropriate fruits! I am not expecting my mango tree to give me leaves to eat. I simply do not want mango leaf salad. I am expecting fruits! God is expecting fruits from you! Don't disappoint Him! Don't anger Him!

CHAPTER 7

Bearing Tares

Another parable put he forth unto them, saying, The kingdom of heaven is likened unto a man which sowed good seed in his field: But while men slept, his enemy came and sowed tares among the wheat, and went his way. But when the blade was sprung up, and brought forth fruit, then ap-peared the tares also. So the servants of the householder came and said unto him, SIR, DIDST NOT THOU SOW GOOD SEED IN THY FIELD? FROM WHENCE THEN HATH IT TARES? He said unto them, an enemy hath done this. The servants said unto him, Wilt thou then that we go and gather them up? But he said, Nay; lest while ye gather up the tares, ye root up also the wheat with them. Let both grow together until the harvest: and in the time of harvest I will say to the reapers, Gather ye together first the tares, and bind them in bundles to burn them: but gather the wheat into my barn.

Matthew 13:24-30

A picture of tares growing together with wheat

There are many things that look like fruit but are actually not fruit. Tares look like fruit. When I first saw a picture of tares, I was amazed at the similarity between the tares and the wheat. Today, there are many things going on in the body of Christ that are best described as tares. They look like wheat but they are tares. They closely resemble the wheat so you need discerning eyes to pick them out.

Today, we have tares that are parading as Christian music. Today, there are tares that are parading as preaching of the gospel. Pastors preach as though they were motivational speakers and bank managers. Motivational speeches and messages that teach on wealth creation are not the same as preaching the gospel.

Teaching someone how to make his first million dollars is not the same as preaching the gospel. However, these speeches make people very happy and have a good and positive psychological ef-fect on the hearers.

Tares are very similar to wheat. The preaching of the gospel is not the practice of psychology. It is the propagation of the good news of the cross of Jesus Christ. We are not ashamed of the gospel of Jesus Christ. It is the gospel of Jesus Christ that has the power to save people and change their lives. Motivational speeches about finance and business do not save the souls of men.

Today, there are many social services going on. The opening of schools, hospitals and universities is not the same as preaching the gospel. Because large churches and rich ministries have all these activities, Christians tend to think that this is the right thing to do. Always remember that tares look like wheat! You cannot eat tares but you can eat wheat. What is the use of these tares that cannot be eaten?

CHAPTER 8

Supernatural Laws of Fruitfulness

Now will I sing to my wellbeloved a song of my beloved touching his vineyard. My wellbeloved hath a vineyard in a very fruitful hill: And he fenced it, and gathered out the stones thereof, and planted it with the choicest vine, and built a tower in the midst of it, and also made a winepress therein: and he looked that it should bring forth grapes, and it brought forth wild grapes.

And now, O inhabitants of Jerusalem, and men of Judah, judge, I pray you, betwixt me and my vineyard. What could have been done more to my vineyard, that I have not done in it? Wherefore, when I looked that it should bring forth grapes, brought it forth wild grapes?

And now go to; I will tell you what I will do to my vineyard: I will take away the hedge thereof, and it shall be eaten up; and break down the wall thereof, and it shall be trodden down: And I will lay it waste: it shall not be pruned, nor digged; but there shall come up briers and thorns: I will also command the clouds that they rain no rain upon it.

For the vineyard of the Lord of hosts is the house of Israel, and the men of Judah his pleasant plant: and he looked for judgment, but behold oppression; for righteousness, but behold a cry.

Isaiah 5:1-7

The story above is a prophetic story that reveals the supernatural laws of fruitfulness. It reveals that there is a supernatural dimension to a life of fruitfulness. There are many supernatural things that happen so that you can bear fruits. In this passage, God reveals all the things that He does on your behalf so that you can be fruitful. If God were not to act, operate and manoeuvre behind the scenes, you would not be able to be fruitful. That is why it is offensive for you to not bear any fruits at all.

1. THE LAW OF THE SUPERNATURAL FENCE.

And he FENCED IT, and gathered out the stones thereof, and planted it with the choicest vine, and built a tower in the midst of it, and also made a winepress therein: and he looked that it should bring forth grapes, and it brought forth wild grapes.

Isaiah 5:2

There is a supernatural fence around you for your fruitfulness.

You may not realise that there is a supernatural fence around you. You could have died long ago from so-called natural and unnatural causes. You may not know that, many times as a child, you were in hospital and your mother thought you would die. All that time, God was protecting you because He knew you would bear fruit.

Do you not know anybody your age or younger who has already died of cancer? I remember a thirty-five-year-old man who developed a strange cancer of the spine. I watched in amazement as he died in the midst of his years. Before he died, he said to me, "If God gives me a second chance, I will serve Him."

There are many people younger than you who have already gone away from this life. There are many accidents that you could have had.

I was once in an accident where I should have died. But I did not die!

I was once in an aeroplane that was struck by lightning but God kept me.

I was once in a plane that almost collided with another plane on the runway but God kept me.

Why did He save me? The law of the supernatural fence was at work!

Why did God protect me from all these things? Because He had in mind the fruits that He wanted me to bear!

God has fruits that He wants you to bear. He has supernaturally placed a fence around you and kept you from death. God has kept you from death by natural causes, unnatural causes and freak incidents.

2. THE LAW OF SUPERNATURAL REMOVAL OF STONES.

And he fenced it, and GATHERED OUT THE STONES thereof, and planted it with the choicest vine, and built a tower in the midst of it, and also made a wine-press therein: and he looked that it should bring forth grapes, and it brought forth wild grapes.

Isaiah 5:2

The stones in this prophetic story speaks of obstacles and hindrances to your fruitfulness. There is a supernatural removal of problems for your fruitfulness.

God Himself has pledged to supernaturally remove the stones that prevent you from being a fruitful field.

The stones have been cleared! If the stone is a circumstance, it will be removed for your sake! If the stone is a person, he will be removed for your sake! If the stone is an authority figure, he will be replaced for your sake! God is on the move to ensure that every impediment in your way is removed.

There is a supernatural removal of problems and difficulties in your life. You are overcoming every blockage in your life! Every administrative, legal, technical or medical obstacle, challenge is being removed by God!

There are many situations that you came out of, victorious! It was not because you were good or clever but because the grace of God worked in you. God was supernaturally removing the stones from the garden so that you could become fruitful. Expect God to supernaturally clear away the barriers in your way!

3. THE LAW OF SUPERNATURAL INVESTMENT.

And he fenced it, and gathered out the stones thereof, and PLANTED IT with the choicest vine, and built a tower in the midst of it, and also made a winepress therein: and he looked that it should bring forth grapes, and it brought forth wild grapes.

Isaiah 5:2

There is a supernatural investment in your life.

God has supernaturally planted the best in you! You may not realise how God has introduced you to some of the best ministers of the gospel. God has planted in you some of the best advice possible. God has invested in you good friends who help you.

When I look at my life, I see that God has invested so much in me. He gave me good people who were good Christians filled with holiness, purity and the love of God to teach me about God. That was God's investment in my life!

God planted His choicest vine in my life and made me come in contact with wonderful pastors, evangelists and teachers of the Word. When I was introduced to Kenneth Hagin and Fred Price, it was God's supernatural way of investing in me.

When I was introduced to a young spiritual mother called Betty who taught me how to have my quiet time, it was God's kindness towards me. When God gave me the parents he gave me, it was His way of investing in me. There is great spiritual investment in your life. It must not be a wasted investment!

4. THE LAW OF THE SUPERNATURAL TOWER.

And he fenced it, and gathered out the stones thereof, and planted it with the choicest vine, and built A TOWER in the midst of it, and also made a winepress therein: and he looked that it should bring forth grapes, and it brought forth wild grapes.

Isaiah 5:2

There is a supernatural tower of security for your fruitfulness.

God has built a tower in your midst! There is a supernatural tower in your midst! That tower contains lookout angels. Some of the angels live on the first floor. Some of the angels live on the second floor and there is always an angel on the top floor. The angel of the Lord encamps around them that fear the Lord (Psalm 34:7). This special security, where God is looking out for you and saving you from the pits of hell, is a special provision from God.

There are spiritual snakes that are seeking to bite you. There are spiritual cobras that are seeking to paralyse you. There are spiritual black mambas that are seeking to terrorise your life. There are spiritual elephants seeking to crush you. There are spiritual lions seeking to terrify you. There are spiritual leopards seeking to jump on you and take you by surprise. There are spiritual hippopotamuses seeking to charm you with lustful displays of fleshly extravagance. There are spiritual insects seeking to transmit disease and death in your life.

When you read your Bible, you discover that all these animals exist in the spirit. God has placed a supernatural tower in your midst. All these attacks, dangers and threats are being warded off from this tower!

41

5. THE LAW OF THE WINEPRESS.

And he fenced it, and gathered out the stones thereof, and planted it with the choicest vine, and built a tower in the midst of it, and also made A WINEPRESS therein: and he looked that it should bring forth grapes, and it brought forth wild grapes.

Isaiah 5:2

There is a supernatural winepress for your fruitfulness.

The wine press speaks of how your fruits will be used. God has supernaturally provided places for you to bear fruit. You are not just going to produce grapes that will go to waste. There is a wine press waiting for your fruits.

Similarly, there are many souls, churches and much work waiting for you to get involved in. God has many things for you to do! There are fields of harvest waiting to receive the fruit of your life and fruit of your ministry.

Indeed, there is a supernatural provision of all things for your fruitfulness. What else can be done to make you fruitful? What else can be said that will make you fruitful?

WHAT COULD HAVE BEEN DONE MORE TO MY VINEYARD, that I have not done in it? Wherefore, when I looked that it should bring forth grapes, brought it forth wild grapes?

Isaiah 5:4

When the harvest fields do not hear from you, it is a great disappointment because a lot has been invested in you.

God is asking you a question today! What else can be done to make you bear fruits that has not been done? A lot has been put into you! This is why there will be a severe judgment on you if you do not bear fruit.

Perhaps you escaped from a war!

Perhaps your friends are in prison today!

Perhaps your other friends are dead!

Perhaps your other friends are in a mental institution!

Here you are alive and well, lifting up holy hands and praising the Lord in church. So much grace has been shown to you! The law of the supernatural fence has worked for you! The law of stone removal has worked for you! The law of the supernatural tower has worked for you. The law of the winepress has worked for you! The fields of harvest are waiting for you! There are towns, cities, countries and nations waiting to hear from you! The winepress is waiting to receive your fruits!

Perhaps you escaped from the Ebola virus!

Perhaps you escaped from the HIV virus!

Perhaps you escaped from the Corona virus pandemic!

Perhaps, you escaped from death!

What more could God have done for you? Is that not the law of the supernatural fence and the law of the supernatural tower at work in your life? It is time to show that you are grateful!

CHAPTER 9

The Rules of Peace
and Fruitfulness

And the fruit of righteousness is sown in peace of them that make peace.

James 3:18

RULE 1: FRUITFULNESS IN MINISTRY IS POSSIBLE ONLY IN AN ENVIRONMENT OF PEACE.

S atan seeks to take away the peace from your life. The fruit of righteousness is always created in an environment of peace. Many pastors are harassed and weary from issues that seek to take away their peace. All these many conflicts serve as a distraction for God's servants. Satan is more aware of this rule of peace than most ministers. You need peace if you want to bear fruit.

And the fruit of righteousness is sown in peace of them that make peace.

James 3:18

Many pastors live in conflict with their spouses not understanding that satan is behind the conflict in their homes. The conflict in your life is intended to take away peace. Once the peace has been taken away, the environment in which you can bear much fruit is destroyed.

Many pastors have quarrels with their wives on Saturdays and Sunday mornings. Demons rise up against the pastor and work through their wives, creating a mysterious weekend conflict in the home. Because the pastor is going to bear the fruit of preaching the Word, his peace is attacked in the home.

Many experienced pastors will learn to avoid conflict in the run-up to great spiritual events.

RULE 2: FRUITFULNESS IN BUILDING IS POSSIBLE ONLY IN AN ENVIRONMENT OF PEACE.

And Solomon sent to Hiram, saying, Thou knowest how that David MY FATHER COULD NOT BUILD an house unto the name of the Lord his God FOR THE WARS WHICH WERE ABOUT HIM ON EVERY SIDE, until the Lord put them under the soles of his feet. But now the Lord my GOD HATH GIVEN ME REST on every side, so that there is neither adversary nor evil occurrent. And, behold, I purpose to build an house unto the name of the Lord my God, as the Lord spake unto David my father, saying, Thy son, whom I will set upon thy throne in thy room, he shall build an house unto my name.

1 Kings 5:2-5

David could not build the house for the Lord because of the conflict that was in his life. David had wars around him on every side. When you have conflict on every side of your life, you cannot build much. It is important to dry out and quench all forms of disloyalty and treachery in your life. When you have quenched the insurgencies and rebellions against your leadership, you will have rest on every side. When you have rest on every side, you will become like Solomon and be able to build great things for God. Solomon was commissioned by the Lord to build the temple because he had the necessary peace.

When I began to teach on loyalty and disloyalty, many people did not understand what I was doing. I was actually destroying the enemies of the church and creating a peaceful environment in the house of God.

Those who leave you, those who pretend, those who are disloyal, those who forget and those who accuse you are the ones who destroy the peace in your life. You must learn to deal with all forms of disloyalty so that you can have an environment of peace! Dangerous sons and ignorant people are destroyers of peace. The influence and power of such people to destroy peace must be broken so that you can have peace.

Perhaps you have not been able to build much for God. It is because you have wars on every side. You are fighting with your wife at home, you are fighting with your in-laws, you are fighting with your assistant pastors, you are fighting with your employees and you are fighting with your financial supporters. These numerous wars will not help you to bear much fruit.

Receive the peace of God! Receive the blessing of loyalty, harmony and faithfulness! Through calmness, peace and tranquillity, you will achieve great fruitfulness!

RULE 3: FRUITFULNESS IN BUSINESS IS POSSIBLE ONLY IN AN ENVIRONMENT OF PEACE.

And Isaac's servants digged in the valley, and found there a well of springing water. And the herdmen of Gerar did STRIVE with Isaac's herdmen, saying, The water is ours: and he called the name of the well Esek; because they STROVE with him. And they digged another well, and STROVE for that also: and he called the name of it Sitnah. And he removed from thence, and digged another well; and for that they STROVE NOT: and he called the name of it Rehoboth; and he said, FOR NOW THE LORD HATH MADE ROOM FOR US, AND WE SHALL BE FRUITFUL IN THE LAND.

Genesis 26:19-22

Isaac was a businessman seeking to prosper in the land. Every attempt to generate water was met with strife, confusion and conflict. He wisely moved away from every conflict until he came to a place where there was no strife. When Isaac had peace, he was able to start on the road of prosperity, expansion and enlargement.

Who are you quarrelling with? Who are you in conflict with? You need peace if you want to experience God's prosperity. Quarrelsome people cannot easily prosper. It is time to make peace and move away from areas of conflict.

CHAPTER 10

The Holy Spirit Makes You a Fruitful Field

Upon the land of my people shall come up thorns and briers; yea, upon all the houses of joy in the joyous city: Because the palaces shall be forsaken; the multitude of the city shall be left; the forts and towers shall be for dens for ever, a joy of wild asses, a pasture of flocks;

UNTIL THE SPIRIT BE POURED UPON US FROM ON HIGH, AND THE WILDERNESS BE A FRUITFUL FIELD, AND THE FRUITFUL FIELD BE COUNTED FOR A FOREST.

Isaiah 32:13-15

The dryness in your life and the fruitlessness in your life are because of the lack of the Holy Spirit in your life.

The influence of the Holy Spirit on your life will make you fruitful. When the Spirit is poured out on you, your life changes and you become fruitful. When you become anointed you become fruitful.

1. The Holy Spirit made Jesus fruitful.

The Spirit of the Lord is upon me, because he hath anointed me to preach the gospel to the poor; he hath sent me to heal the brokenhearted, to preach deliverance to the captives, and recovering of sight to the blind, to set at liberty them that are bruised, to preach the acceptable year of the Lord.

Luke 4:18-19

The Holy Spirit will turn the wilderness into a fruitful field. When the Holy Spirit came on Jesus, He went about preaching the gospel. Many people were saved. Before the Holy Spirit came on Jesus, He was an unknown carpenter locked up in Nazareth. The Holy Spirit was the key that turned Jesus into the Saviour of the world. The Holy Spirit will turn every wilderness into a fruitful field.

2. The Holy Spirit made the disciples fruitful.

And suddenly there came a sound from heaven as of a rushing mighty wind, and it filled all the house where they were sitting. And there appeared unto them cloven tongues like as of fire, and it sat upon each of them. AND THEY WERE ALL FILLED WITH THE HOLY GHOST, AND BEGAN TO SPEAK WITH OTHER TONGUES, as the Spirit gave them utterance…. Peter, standing up with the eleven, lifted up his voice, and said unto them, Ye men of Judaea, and all ye that dwell at Jerusalem, be this known unto you, and hearken to my words: …

Then they that gladly received his word were baptized: AND THE SAME DAY THERE WERE ADDED UNTO THEM ABOUT THREE THOUSAND SOULS.

Acts 2:2-4, 14, 41

The Holy Spirit will turn the wilderness into a fruitful field! The disciples were a prophetic and barren wilderness till the Holy Spirit came upon them! When the Holy Spirit came on the disciples, they started preaching about Jesus and offering salvation to the world.

When the Holy Spirit fell on the disciples, they became fruitful. Silent, depressed and discouraged apostles of Jesus Christ became fruitful soul winners when the Spirit of God came on them on the Day of Pentecost.

3. The Holy Spirit made Elisha a fruitful field.

So he departed thence, and found Elisha the son of Shaphat, who was plowing with twelve yoke of oxen before him, and he with the twelfth: and Elijah passed by him, and cast his mantle upon him.

1 Kings 19:19

And he took the mantle of Elijah that fell from him, and smote the waters, and said, where is the Lord God of Elijah? And when he also had smitten the waters, they parted hither and thither: and Elisha went over.

2 Kings 2:14

The Holy Spirit will turn the wilderness into a fruitful field! Elisha was an unknown shepherd following cows across the fields of the Middle East. When the mantle of the Holy Spirit came on him, he turned into a mighty prophet who bore much fruit and did wonders for God. Everyone in the world knows about Elisha today. Elisha bore twice as much fruit as Elijah. What brought about the great change in Elisha? What made Elisha fruitful? It was the mantle of the Holy Spirit that came upon him.

4. The Holy Spirit made Saul into a fruitful field.

> Then Samuel took a vial of oil, and poured it upon his
> head, and kissed him, and said, is it not because the Lord
> hath anointed thee to be captain over his inheritance? ...
> And the Spirit of the Lord will come upon thee, and thou
> shalt prophesy with them, and shalt be turned into another
> man....
>
> And when they came thither to the hill, behold, a company
> of prophets met him; and the Spirit of God came upon
> him, and he prophesied among them. And it came to pass,
> when all that knew him beforetime saw that, behold, he
> prophesied among the prophets, then the people said one
> to another, What is this that is come unto the son of Kish?
> Is Saul also among the prophets?
>
> 1 Samuel 10:1, 6, 10-11

The Holy Spirit will turn the wilderness into a fruitful field.
Saul was an unknown young man in Israel. There was nothing
unusual about him till Samuel anointed him. Samuel declared
that he was now anointed to be a king. Today, we all know about
Saul because the Holy Spirit came upon Him. The Holy Spirit
constantly turns wildernesses into fruitful fields.

5. The Holy Spirit turned Isaiah into a fruitful field.

> The Spirit of the Lord God is upon me; because the Lord
> hath anointed me to preach good tidings unto the meek;
> he hath sent me to bind up the brokenhearted, to proclaim
> liberty to the captives, and the opening of the prison to
> them that are bound;
>
> Isaiah 61:1

Isaiah declared that the Spirit of the Lord had come upon him
and had turned him into a preacher of good news. Isaiah was
enabled to bind up the broken-hearted and proclaim liberty to
the captives.

Isaiah was able to set captives free because the Holy Spirit was upon him. Isaiah had suddenly turned into a fruitful field because the Holy Spirit was upon him.

CHAPTER 11

Enemies of Fruitfulness

Another parable put he forth unto them, saying, The kingdom of heaven is likened unto a man which sowed good seed in his field: But while men slept, his enemy came and sowed tares among the wheat, and went his way. But when the blade was sprung up, and brought forth fruit, then appeared the tares also. So the servants of the householder came and said unto him, Sir, didst not thou sow good seed in thy field? from whence then hath it tares? He said unto them, An enemy hath done this. The servants said unto him, Wilt thou then that we go and gather them up? But he said, Nay; lest while ye gather up the tares, ye root up also the wheat with them. Let both grow together until the harvest: and in the time of harvest I will say to the reapers, Gather ye together first the tares, and bind them in bundles to burn them: but gather the wheat into my barn.

Matthew 13:24-30

Vhen you attempt to be fruitful, there will always be enemies of your fruitfulness. There will be things that will rise up to quench you! It is important to fight against all the enemies of your fruitfulness. You will notice from the scripture above that tares were the greatest challenge to the fruitfulness of the wheat.

How the Enemy Fights Your Fruitfulness

1. The enemy fights your fruitfulness through leviathan, the crooked serpent.

In that day the Lord with his sore and great and strong sword shall punish LEVIATHAN THE PIERCING SERPENT, even LEVIATHAN THAT CROOKED SERPENT; and he SHALL SLAY THE DRAGON that is in the sea. In that day sing ye unto her, a vineyard of red wine. I the Lord do keep it; I will water it every moment: lest any hurt it, I will keep it night and day.

Fury is not in me: who would set the briers and thorns against me in battle? I would go through them, I would burn them together. Or let him take hold of my strength, that he may make peace with me; and he shall make peace with me.

HE SHALL CAUSE THEM THAT COME OF JACOB TO TAKE ROOT: ISRAEL SHALL BLOSSOM AND BUD, AND FILL THE FACE OF THE WORLD WITH FRUIT.

Isaiah 27:1-6

When leviathan is pierced through, Israel will blossom and fill the face of the earth with fruit!

We all know that the devil is the old serpent. There are different kinds of serpents though. Leviathan is the crooked serpent. Leviathan is the piercing serpent! The crooked serpent seeks to make everything about your life crooked and corrupt. Whenever there is corruption, fruitfulness is not possible. Many people are unable to bear fruit because of the crookedness in their lives.

Over the years I have observed that missionaries who are unable to bear fruit have some crookedness tucked away in the secret places. I remember a young man whom we sent to the mission field. We sent every possible support to him. He was given everything he asked for. At one point he asked for thousands of dollars to buy some equipment. Indeed, thousands of dollars were spent on him. But the mission never flourished. In the end he was brought back home.

Later on, it was discovered that he was actually a big-time thief and criminal. It was also discovered that he had two families; one seen family and one unseen family.

Leviathan is the crooked serpent that causes all things to be crooked. Crookedness takes away your fruitfulness! Watch barren and fruitless pastors closely! Watch barren and fruitless Christians closely! Leviathan is probably hiding in there somewhere! You will notice that when leviathan was pierced through Israel blossomed and filled the face of the earth with fruit.

2. The enemy fights your fruitfulness through the spirit of leviathan, the piercing serpent.

Leviathan is the piercing serpent that causes hurts and offences. Do not be overcome by the piercing strikes of leviathan. Don't be hurt! Don't be unforgiving! Don't be bitter! The piercing works of leviathan cause offence all the time.

Hurts and offences are reasons why people become fruitless. Most human beings are hurt about something. Most human beings have a good reason to be hurt. Leviathan capitalizes on our tendency to be offended and inflicts more and more piercing wounds in people's hearts.

These piercing leviathan wounds cause barrenness and fruitlessness to engulf Christians. Jesus said that offences would surely come! (Matthew 18:7) Offences are stumbling blocks that cause people to fall flat on their faces and stop moving forward. Many people are flat on their faces, unable to bear fruit anymore because of their hurts. The hurts, offences and stumbling blocks have brought them to a place of barrenness.

3. **The enemy fights your fruitfulness by devouring your fruits as soon as they are born.**

And his tail drew the third part of the stars of heaven, and did cast them to the earth: and THE DRAGON STOOD BEFORE THE WOMAN WHICH WAS READY TO BE DELIVERED, for to devour her child as soon as it was born.

Revelation 12:4

The dragon was well-positioned to swallow up the child of the woman. This is the classic position of the enemy: ready to swallow up your fruits.

Jesus wants us to bear fruit that will abide. Satan wants to swallow up all the young pastors with pornography, sex and homosexuality. Satan wants to devour all the fruits of the ministry.

The beginning of your real strength is when you have fruits of sons and daughters in the ministry. Jacob described his first-born son as the beginning of his strength and might. Indeed, the beginning of your strength and the beginning of your might is when you have fruits of sons and daughters in the ministry.

Reuben, thou art my firstborn, my might, and the beginning of my strength, the excellency of dignity, and the excellency of power:

Genesis 49:3

CHAPTER 12

Sacrifice: The Key to Fruitfulness

And Jesus answered them, saying, the hour is come, that the Son of man should be glorified. Verily, verily, I say unto you, except a corn of wheat FALL into the ground and DIE, it abideth alone: but if it die, it bringeth forth much FRUIT.

John 12:23-24

Without sacrifice there will be no fruit! Many people have knowledge. Many people are learned but simply do not have fruit.

Becoming an effective and fruitful minister is not just by passing exams or acquiring knowledge. There is a need for Christians to rise up and pay the price for bearing fruit.

Jesus Christ came to this world and preached many wonderful things to us. He could have ended His ministry without making a sacrifice. Indeed, there would have been no lasting fruit. Jesus Christ went to the cross and gave His life for all of us. By giving His life and releasing His blood, the power of fruitfulness was unleashed.

Today, Jesus Christ bears fruit as far as in Asia, Africa, Europe and the ends of the world. There is no part of this globe where you cannot find Christians.

The Christian church is not a para-military organisation that is forcing entire populations to adhere to a faith. Christianity is a religion that you join out of your free will. You can come and you can go as you wish. Yet, millions want to follow Jesus Christ and serve Him. That is the power of fruitfulness. That power to be fruitful was released at the cross. The cross is the power of God unto salvation.

You may be able to parrot many verses from the Bible. You may have passed many exams. You may have read many books. But until you sacrifice, you will be alone and fruitless.

Except a corn of wheat fall into the ground and die it abides alone (John 12:24). It is time to fall into the ground and pay the price or you will forever be fruitless and barren in Christ.

CHAPTER 13

Don't Waste Your Goods!

And he said also unto his disciples, there was a certain rich man, which had a steward; and THE SAME WAS ACCUSED UNTO HIM THAT HE HAD WASTED HIS GOODS. And he called him, and said unto him, how is it that I hear this of thee? Give an account of thy stewardship; for thou mayest be no longer steward. Then the steward said within himself, what shall I do? For my lord taketh away from me the stewardship: I cannot dig; to beg I am ashamed. I am resolved what to do, that, when I am put out of the stewardship, they may receive me into their houses. So he called every one of his lord's debtors unto him, and said unto the first, how much owest thou unto my lord? And he said, An hundred measures of oil. And he said unto him, Take thy bill, and sit down quickly, and write fifty. Then said he to another, And how much owest thou? And he said, An hundred measures of wheat. And he said unto him, Take thy bill, and write fourscore. And the lord commended the unjust steward, because he had done wisely: for the children of this world are in their generation wiser than the children of light.

Luke 16:1-8

Your life is an opportunity to be fruitful. You will never live again! You will never celebrate the same birthday twice! Every time you pass a milestone, remember that you will never go back.

In this story, a report was given to the master that the disciple had wasted his goods. Today, the goods you have are the time and life God has given you. Your years are advancing! Your youthfulness is ending! Your hair is changing colour! Soon the years will be gone and you will say, "I wasted my life."

Rise up now and be wise! The wisdom that is from above is to be fruitful!

But THE WISDOM THAT IS FROM ABOVE is first pure, then peaceable, gentle, and easy to be intreated, FULL OF MERCY AND GOOD FRUITS, without partiality, and without hypocrisy.

James 3:17

The wise man will be full of good fruits.

The master decided to terminate the appointment of his servant because his servant was wasting his goods. Jesus may decide to terminate your appointment with life because you are wasting the gifts and time that He gave you.

Rise up and be fruitful! There are too many warnings about fruitlessness. God has spoken to you! You must be fruitful! You must use what He has given you!

Conclusion

The Holy Spirit has led you to read this book on fruitfulness. Being fruitful is the greatest wisdom that you can ever have on this earth! It is the purpose of God and it is the only reason why you are alive.

To the making of many books there is no end! With these few words, I admonish all my children!